D1572850

LANGUAGE ARTS

EXPLORER JUNIOR

How to Write a News Article

by Cecilia Minden
and Kate Roth

CHERRY LAKE PUBLISHING · ANN ARBOR, MICHIGAN

Published in the United States of America by Cherry Lake Publishing
Ann Arbor, Michigan
www.cherrylakepublishing.com

Content Adviser: Jeannette Mancilla-Martinez, EdD, Assistant Professor of
Literacy, Language, and Culture, University of Illinois at Chicago

Design and Illustration: The Design Lab

Photo Credits: Page 4, ©archana bhartia/Shutterstock, Inc.; page 8,
©Jacek ChabraszewskiDreamstime.com; page 11, ©littleny/Shutterstock,
Inc.; page 20, ©iStockphoto.com/bowdenimages.

Copyright ©2012 by Cherry Lake Publishing
All rights reserved. No part of this book may be reproduced or utilized in
any form or by any means without written permission from the publisher.

Library of Congress Cataloging-in-Publication Data
Minden, Cecilia.
  How to write a news article/by Cecilia Minden and Kate Roth.
    p. cm.
  Includes bibliographical references and index.
  ISBN 978-1-61080-308-3 (lib. bdg.)—ISBN 978-1-61080-313-7
(e-book)—ISBN 978-1-61080-318-2 (pbk.)
1. Reportage literature—Technique—Juvenile literature. 2. Nonfiction novel—
Technique—Juvenile literature. 3. Exposition (Rhetoric)—Juvenile literature.
4. Creative writing—Juvenile literature. I. Roth, Kate. II. Title.
  PN3377.5.R45M54 2011
  808'.042—dc23   2011030945

Cherry Lake Publishing would like to acknowledge
the work of The Partnership for 21st Century Skills.
Please visit www.21stcenturyskills.org
for more information.

Printed in the United States of America
Corporate Graphics Inc.
January 2012
CLSP10

Table of Contents

CHAPTER ONE

Read All About It!

Reading newspapers is a great way to learn what's going on in the world.

We can learn new things by reading news **articles**. News articles can tell us about events in our school or town. They can also tell us about events far away. Articles may be about events that just happened. They might be about events that are about to happen.

News articles give us details and facts that we might not have known. People who write the news are called **reporters**. Let's give reporting a try!

You can write about recent events.

News articles must be **current**. They should be of interest to many readers. "Jim took a spelling test" isn't news. "Every third grader in the city scored 100 on spelling tests for 10 weeks in a row" is news. This would be of interest to many people. That's what makes it news.

Reporters are good listeners. They come up with ideas for articles by listening to what people are saying. Are most of your friends talking about the same thing? Chances are it would make a good news story.

Reporters often use computers to record their stories.

Choose Your Story

In this activity you will choose the topic for your article.

HERE'S WHAT YOU'LL NEED:
- Pencil
- Paper

INSTRUCTIONS:
1. Think about current events at your school or in your town.
2. Think about topics all your friends are talking about.
3. Make a list of ideas for your news article.
4. Choose one to write about.

To get a copy of this activity, visit www.cherrylakepublishing.com/activities.

WHAT ARE PEOPLE TALKING ABOUT?
- School book fair
- Winter music concert
- Field trip to the zoo
- This week's snowstorm
- Spelling bee winners

CHAPTER TWO

Get the Facts

Talk to others to get ideas for stories.

Reporters do research to get the facts for their articles. They talk to people. They ask *who, what, where, when, why,* and *how* questions. They write down the answers to those questions.

Make sure your news articles contain facts. Two people or groups might not agree about the facts. Be sure to talk to both sides. That way readers can make an informed choice about the topic. Use at least two **sources** of information to **verify** the facts you gather.

ACTIVITY

Gather Information

In this activity you will do research to get the facts for your article.

HERE'S WHAT YOU'LL NEED:
- Pencil
- Paper

INSTRUCTIONS:
1. Do research to find facts that answer these questions: who, what, where, when, why, and how.
2. Talk to people who were involved in the event. Write down exactly what they say.
3. Ask an adult to help you find current information online.

To get a copy of this activity, visit www.cherrylakepublishing.com/activities.

WHO? Kids from my school including Sam, Emma, Taylor

WHAT? no school because of snow

WHEN? first Tuesday in February

WHERE? our city

WHY? 18 inches of snow kept everyone home

HOW DID KIDS SPEND THE DAY?
- Sam went sledding and drank hot chocolate.
- Emma read books and played games.
- Taylor built a snow fort and had a snowball fight.

Building Your Article

Plan your article carefully before you type it up.

Next you need to think about how to organize your article. News articles begin with a **lead**. The lead is a sentence that gets your readers' attention. Follow your lead with two or three paragraphs about what happened. This is the **body** of your article. Finally, write the conclusion. This is how the story ends.

Here is how one well-known nursery rhyme might work as a news article:

There was an old woman who lived in a shoe. **(the lead)**

She had so many children, she didn't know what to do. **(the body)**

She gave them some broth without any bread, **(the body)**

Then kissed them all gently and put them to bed. **(the conclusion)**

Organize Your Article

In this activity you will organize your article.

HERE'S WHAT YOU'LL NEED:
- Pencil
- Paper

INSTRUCTIONS:
1. Organize your research into the different parts of your news article. You'll have a lead, the body paragraphs, and a conclusion.
2. Write a lead sentence to get your reader's attention.
3. List the facts that will go in each paragraph.
4. Plan your conclusion.

To get a copy of this activity, visit www.cherrylakepublishing.com/activities.

LEAD: Kids at Jefferson School got a big surprise on Tuesday.

FACTS FOR PARAGRAPH #1:
- What happened?
- There were 18 inches of snow.
- School was closed.

FACTS FOR PARAGRAPH #2:
- How did kids spend the day?
- Sam went sledding and drank hot chocolate.
- Emma was sick. She stayed home and read books and played games.
- Taylor built a snow fort and had a snowball fight with friends.

CONCLUSION: More snow is expected later this week.

CHAPTER FOUR

Here's the Story

Your goal as a reporter is to interest your readers. You do this by writing in an **engaging** way. A news article should be more than a list of facts. Don't just tell what happened. Try to tell the story using the words of people you interviewed.

ACTIVITY

Write the News Article

In this activity you will write your article in an engaging way.

HERE'S WHAT YOU'LL NEED:
- Pencil
- Paper

CONTINUED

To get a copy of this activity, visit www.cherrylakepublishing.com/activities.

(WRITE THE NEWS ARTICLE CONTINUED)

INSTRUCTIONS

1. Use the plan you created in the previous activity as a guide.
2. Write a lead sentence to get your readers' attention.
3. Write each paragraph. Use the facts in your plan to write at least three sentences for each paragraph.
4. Make your writing engaging. Include exactly what people said. Try to include fun facts.
5. Write your conclusion.

The kids at Jefferson School got a big surprise on Tuesday. They woke up to 18 inches of snow. It covered cars, yards, and roads. The mayor asked everyone to stay home and off the streets. All the schools were closed.

Kids from Jefferson School spent their day in different ways. Second-grade student Sam Cook went sledding in the park. "We kept warm with Mom's hot chocolate," said Sam. First-grader Emma Watts had a cold. She had to stay inside. She spent the day reading and playing games with her sisters. "We had a lot of fun," said Emma. Taylor Bloom is a third-grader. He and his friends built snow forts. They had snowball fights all afternoon.

More snow is expected this week. Kids won't be upset about that. "Snow days are awesome!" declared Taylor.

CHAPTER FIVE

Making Headlines

A catchy headline will get readers' attention. A headline is the title of your news article. A headline tells a story in just a few words. It helps readers decide whether or not to read your story.

You may want to add a picture to your story. A picture can help draw in readers. A caption usually appears under the picture.

Pictures help the reader relive the event.

A caption is one or two sentences that describe what is happening in the picture. Include the names of any people in the picture.

Add a Headline and Pictures

In this activity you will write a headline and illustrate your article.

HERE'S WHAT YOU'LL NEED:
- Pencil
- Crayons or colored pencils
- A photograph of the event

INSTRUCTIONS:
1. Write a headline for your news article.
2. Choose a photograph of the event or draw a picture to illustrate your topic.
3. Are there people in your photograph? If so, ask their permission to be included.
4. Write a caption for your picture.

To get a copy of this activity, visit www.cherrylakepublishing.com/activities.

KIDS TRADE SCHOOL FOR SLEDS

SOME KIDS WENT SLEDDING ON THE SNOW DAY.

The kids at Jefferson School got a big surprise on Tuesday. They woke up to 18 inches of snow. It covered cars, yards, and roads. The mayor asked everyone to stay home and off the streets. All the schools were closed.

Kids from Jefferson School spent their day in different ways. Second-grade student Sam Cook went sledding in the park. "We kept warm with Mom's hot chocolate," said Sam. First-grader Emma Watts had a cold. She had to stay inside. She spent the day reading and playing games with her sisters. "We had a lot of fun," said Emma. Taylor Bloom is a third-grader. He and his friends built snow forts. They had snowball fights all afternoon.

More snow is expected this week. Kids won't be upset about that. "Snow days are awesome!" declared Taylor.

CHAPTER SIX

Your Own Byline

Reporters put their names under the headline. This is called a **byline**. Anyone reading the story will know who wrote it.

Maybe someday you will be a news reporter for a big newspaper. Then we will read stories with your byline!

Share your articles with your friends and family!

STOP!
DON'T WRITE
IN THE BOOK!

To get a copy of this activity, visit
www.cherrylakepublishing.com/activities.

ACTIVITY

Did I Choose a Newsworthy Topic?

Read your news article. Carefully check everything one more time. Ask yourself these questions:

☐ YES ☐ NO   Did I answer the questions: who, what, where, when, why, and how?

☐ YES ☐ NO   Did I begin my news article with a lead?

☐ YES ☐ NO   Did I include facts in the body?

☐ YES ☐ NO   Did I end the article with a conclusion?

☐ YES ☐ NO   Did I include a catchy headline?

☐ YES ☐ NO   Did I include an illustration with a caption?

☐ YES ☐ NO   Did I use my byline?

☐ YES ☐ NO   Did I use correct spelling and grammar?

Glossary

articles (AHR-ti-kuhlz) pieces of writing published in newspapers, magazines, or online

body (BAH-dee) the main text of an article

byline (BYE-line) a line at the beginning of an article that gives the author's name

caption (KAP-shuhn) a short description that appears with an illustration

conclusion (kuhn-KLOO-zhuhn) the end of something

current (KUR-uhnt) happening now

engaging (en-GAY-jing) interesting or entertaining

headline (HED-line) the title of an article in a newspaper, magazine, or Web site

illustrate (IL-uh-strayt) add or include pictures

lead (LEED) the first sentence of a news article

reporters (ri-POR-turz) people who gather and report the news

sources (SORS-ez) people who provide information

verify (VER-uh-fye) to confirm that a fact is true

For More Information

BOOKS

Cupp, Dave, and Cecilia Minden. *TV-Station Secrets*. Mankato, MN: The Child's World, 2009.

Flora, Sherrill B., and Jo Browning-Wroe. *The Fairy Tale Times: 10 Fairy Tales Rewritten as High-Interest Front Page News Articles*. Minneapolis: Key Education Publishing, 2006.

WEB SITES

ReadWriteThink Printing Press
interactives.mped.org/view_interactive.aspx?id=110&title=
Use this Web site to create your own newspaper.

Time for Kids
www.timeforkids.com
Read news articles about many interesting topics at this *Time* magazine Web site.

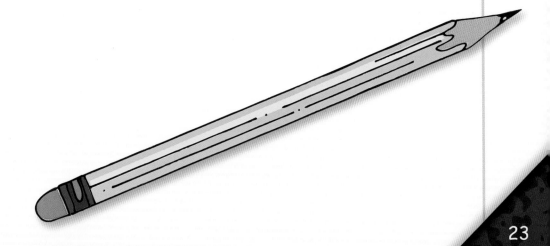

Index

About the Authors

Cecilia Minden, PhD, is the former director of the Language and Literacy Program at Harvard Graduate School of Education. She earned her doctorate from the University of Virginia. While at Harvard, Dr. Minden also taught several writing courses. Her research focuses on early literacy skills and developing phonics curriculums. She is now a full-time literacy consultant and the author of more than 100 books for children. Dr. Minden lives with her family in Chapel Hill, North Carolina. She likes to write early in the morning while the house is still quiet.

Kate Roth has a doctorate from Harvard University in language and literacy and a master's degree from Columbia University Teachers College in curriculum and teaching. Her work focuses on writing instruction in the primary grades. She has taught kindergarten, first grade, and Reading Recovery. She has also instructed hundreds of teachers from around the world in early literacy practices. She lives in Shanghai, China, with her husband and three children, ages 3, 7, and 10. Together they do a lot of writing to stay in touch with friends and family and to record their experiences.